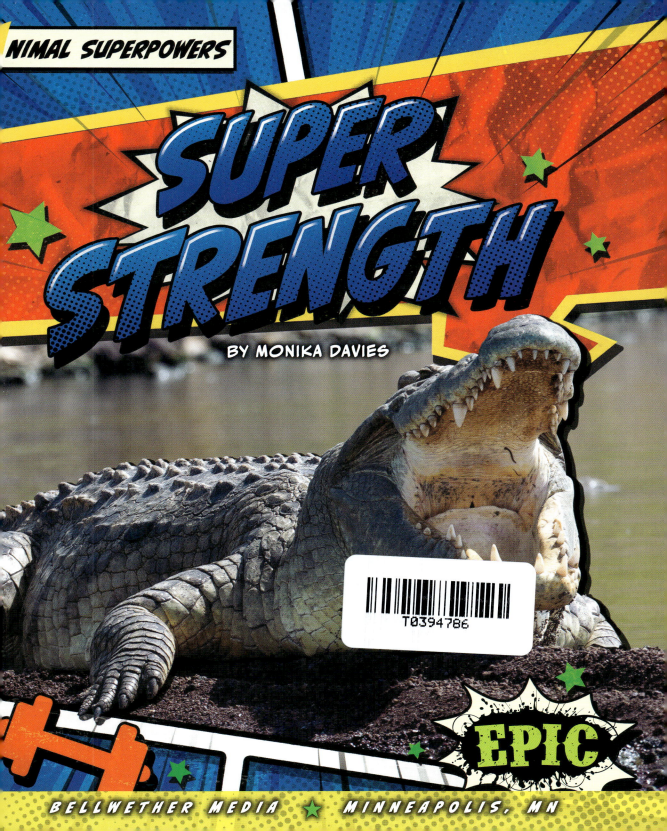

EPIC

EPIC BOOKS are no ordinary books. They burst with intense action, high-speed heroics, and shadows of the unknown. Are you ready for an Epic adventure?

This edition first published in 2026 by Bellwether Media, Inc.

No part of this publication may be reproduced in whole or in part without written permission of the publisher. For information regarding permission, write to Bellwether Media, Inc., Attention: Permissions Department, 3500 American Blvd W, Suite 150, Bloomington, MN 55431.

Library of Congress Cataloging-in-Publication Data

LC record for Super Strength available at: https://lccn.loc.gov/2025021813

Text copyright © 2026 by Bellwether Media, Inc. EPIC and associated logos are trademarks and/or registered trademarks of Bellwether Media, Inc. Bellwether Media is a division of FlutterBee Education Group.

Editor: Rachael Barnes   Designer: Gabriel Hilger

Printed in the United States of America, North Mankato, MN.

TABLE OF CONTENTS

STRENGTH IN FLIGHT 4

THE EPIC EAGLE 6

THE POWERHOUSE
ELEPHANT 10

THE FORCEFUL
CROCODILE 14

THE STRONGEST BEETLE ... 18

GLOSSARY...............................22

TO LEARN MORE 23

INDEX...24

STRENGTH IN FLIGHT

An eagle spots **prey** in a tree. It flies away with a huge meal!

Eagles are one of many animals with super strength. Some animals are giant. Others are tiny. They are strong in different ways.

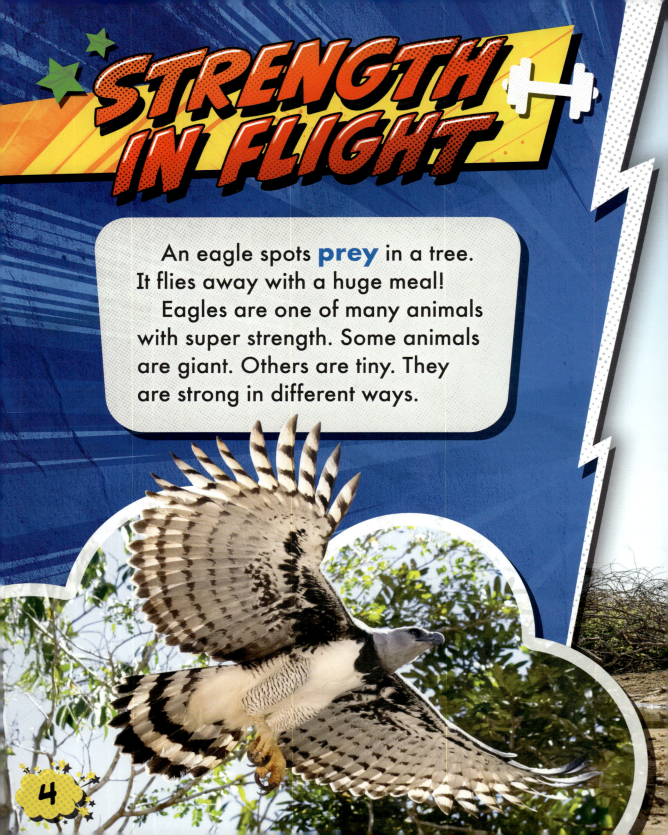

THE EPIC EAGLE

TALONS

Harpy eagles are a **rare** sight in the wild. They hunt and nest in **rain forests**.

Harpy eagles use their strength to hunt. They can grab monkeys from trees.

LONG TALONS

THICK LEGS

POWER LIFTING IN ACTION!
POWERFUL WINGS

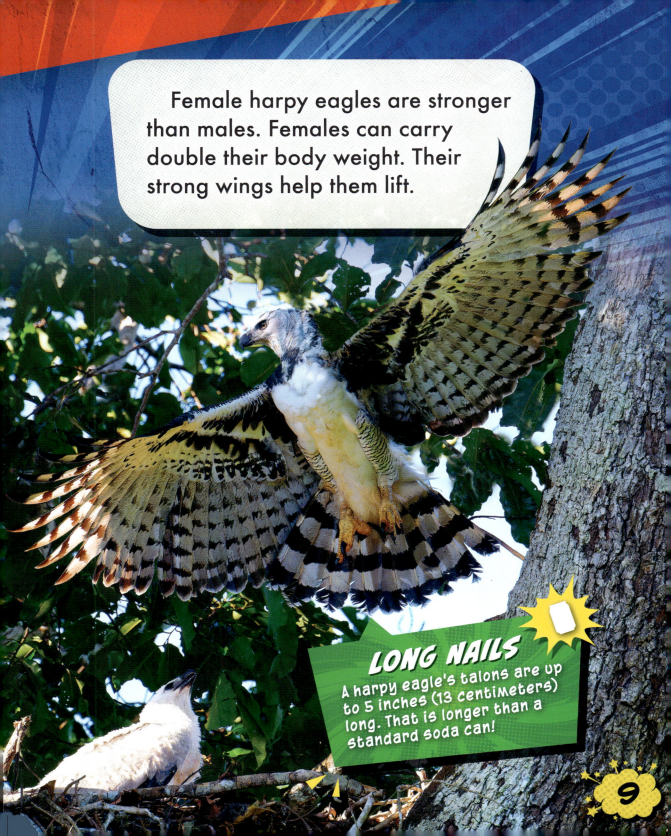

Female harpy eagles are stronger than males. Females can carry double their body weight. Their strong wings help them lift.

LONG NAILS
A harpy eagle's talons are up to 5 inches (13 centimeters) long. That is longer than a standard soda can!

THE POWERHOUSE ELEPHANT

HERD

African bush elephants gather in **herds**. They can push over trees to get food.

10

Their long trunks are strong. They can lift over 700 pounds (318 kilograms)!

AFRICAN BUSH ELEPHANT

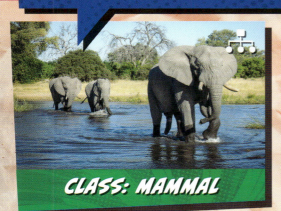

CLASS: MAMMAL

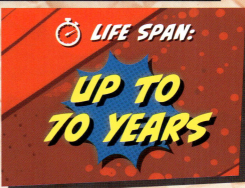

LIFE SPAN: UP TO 70 YEARS

STATUS IN THE WILD

| LEAST CONCERN | NEAR THREATENED | VULNERABLE | ENDANGERED | CRITICALLY ENDANGERED | EXTINCT IN THE WILD | EXTINCT |

RANGE

Elephants may sleep standing up. Their strong legs hold up their body weight. Males can weigh up to 15,000 pounds (6,804 kilograms)!

TRUNK

TOUGH TUSKS

Elephants have tusks. Tusks are long teeth. Male elephants grow tusks that are up to 10 feet (3 meters) long!

TUSK

Male elephants also use their strength to fight each other. The winner leads their herd.

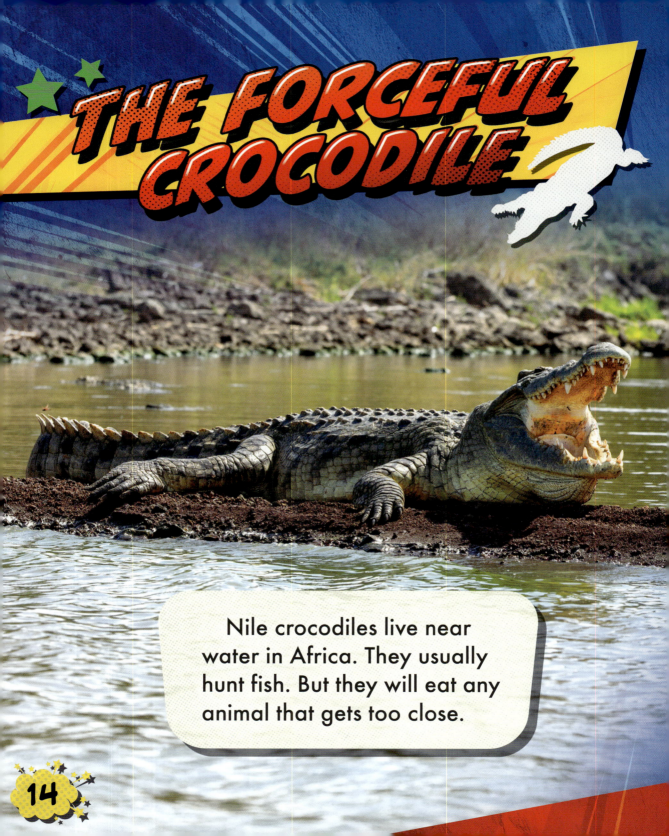

THE FORCEFUL CROCODILE

Nile crocodiles live near water in Africa. They usually hunt fish. But they will eat any animal that gets too close.

These crocodiles wait for their next meal. They quietly **lurk** underwater.

NILE CROCODILE

CLASS: REPTILE

LIFE SPAN:

UP TO 70 YEARS

STATUS IN THE WILD

| LEAST CONCERN | NEAR THREATENED | VULNERABLE | ENDANGERED | CRITICALLY ENDANGERED | EXTINCT IN THE WILD | EXTINCT |

RANGE

HUMAN VS. CROCODILE

Nile crocodiles have the world's strongest bite. Their bite force is 30 times stronger than a human's!

Nile crocodiles leap out of the water. Their jaws grab and lock onto their prey.

They pull their prey underwater. There is no escape from a Nile crocodile's superpowered bite!

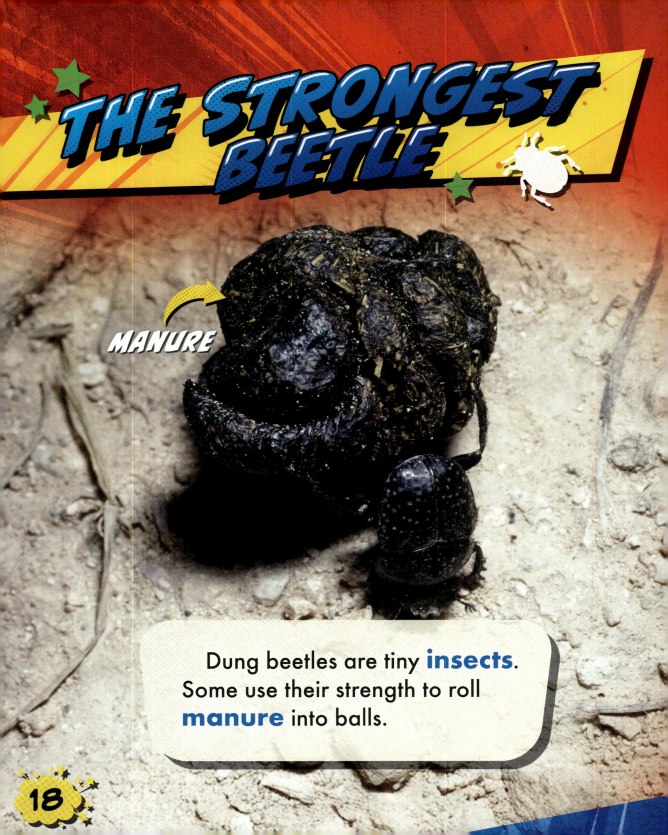

THE STRONGEST BEETLE

MANURE

Dung beetles are tiny **insects**. Some use their strength to roll **manure** into balls.

Adult beetles eat the manure. The balls are a safe place to lay their eggs.

HORNED DUNG BEETLE

CLASS: INSECT

LIFE SPAN: UP TO 3 YEARS

STATUS IN THE WILD

| LEAST CONCERN | NEAR THREATENED | VULNERABLE | ENDANGERED | CRITICALLY ENDANGERED | EXTINCT IN THE WILD | EXTINCT |

RANGE

Horned dung beetles have strong legs to dig and push. They can move objects that are over 1,000 times their body weight!

THE STRONGEST

Horned dung beetles are the world's strongest animal! They can carry a lot for their size.

Super strength comes in all shapes and sizes.

GLOSSARY

herds—groups of animals that live together

insects—small animals with six legs and hard outer bodies; an insect's body is divided into three parts.

lurk—to wait in a hidden place

manure—solid waste from animals

predators—animals that hunt other animals for food

prey—animals that are hunted by other animals for food

rain forests—thick, green forests that receive a lot of rain

rare—not common

talons—long claws on birds

TO LEARN MORE

AT THE LIBRARY

Austen, Lily. *Strongest Animals*. Minneapolis, Minn.: Jump!, 2025.

Kenney, Karen Latchana. *Harpy Eagles*. Minneapolis, Minn.: Bellwether Media, 2021.

Levy, Janey. *Nile Crocodiles Bite!* New York, N.Y.: Gareth Stevens Publishing, 2021.

ON THE WEB

FACTSURFER

Factsurfer.com gives you a safe, fun way to find more information.

1. Go to www.factsurfer.com.

2. Enter "super strength" into the search box and click 🔍.

3. Select your book cover to see a list of related content.

INDEX

Africa, 14
African bush elephants, 10, 11, 12, 13
bite, 16, 17
dung beetles, 18, 19, 20, 21
eggs, 19
females, 9
fight, 13
food, 4, 10, 15
harpy eagles, 4, 6, 7, 8, 9
herds, 10, 13
horned dung beetles, 19, 20, 21
hunt, 6, 8, 14
insects, 18
jaws, 16
jaws in action, 17
legs, 12, 20
lurk, 15

males, 9, 12, 13
manure, 18, 19
Nile crocodiles, 14, 15, 16, 17
power lifting in action, 8
predators, 7
prey, 4, 8, 14, 16, 17
rain forests, 6
range, 7, 11, 15, 19
size, 4, 9, 13, 20, 21
sleep, 12
talons, 6, 7, 9
tree, 4, 8, 10
trunks, 11, 12
tusks, 13
underwater, 15, 17
weight, 9, 11, 12, 20
wings, 9

The images in this book are reproduced through the courtesy of: ArtushFoto, front cover; Przemek Klos, p. 3; Alves-Silva K. R, p. 4; Mark Hunter, p. 5 (elephant); piemags/ nature/ Alamy Stock Photo, p. 5 (beetle); Nature Picture Library/ Alamy Stock Photo, p. 6; Adrian, p. 7 (inset); MarcusVDT, p. 7 (class: bird); NTCo, p. 8 (long talons); Sergi Reboredo/ Alamy Stock Photo, p. 8 (thick legs); Jiang Chunsheng/ Wikipedia, p. 8 (powerful wings); GABRIELLE WEISE, p. 9; Andreanita/ Alamy Stock Photo, p. 10; Ludwig Endres, p. 11 (inset); stuporter, p. 11 (class: mammal); Alexandra Giese, p. 12; Cheryl Ramalho, p. 13; Artush, p. 14; Hanlie Fourie/ Alamy Stock Photo, p. 15 (inset); Martin Mecnarowski, p. 15 (class: reptile); USO, pp. 16-17; Photodynamic, p. 17 (strong jaw); Renato Granieri/ Alamy Stock Photo, p. 17 (powerful bite); Premaphotos/ Minden, p. 18; blickwinkel/ Alamy Stock Photo, pp. 19 (inset), 20; Lee Cain/ Wikipedia, p. 19 (class: insect); WHPics, p. 21; andreanita, p. 22.